The Art of Selling Your Original Masterpiece: A Comprehensive Guide for Artists

Chapter 1: Introduction to Selling Your Art
- Understanding the market for original artwork
- Identifying your target audience
- Setting realistic goals and expectations

Chapter 2: Building Your Brand as an Artist
- Crafting your unique artistic identity
- Establishing an online presence
- Networking and collaborating with other artists and galleries

Chapter 3: Creating Marketable Artwork
- Developing your artistic style
- Experimenting with different mediums and techniques
- Balancing creativity with commercial appeal

Chapter 4: Pricing Your Artwork
- Factors to consider when pricing your art
- Strategies for pricing your work competitively
- Negotiating sales and discounts

Chapter 5: Marketing and Promotion
- Utilizing social media platforms effectively
- Building an email list and newsletter
- Leveraging art shows, exhibitions, and galleries

Chapter 6: Selling Online
- Setting up an e-commerce website
- Utilizing online marketplaces like Etsy, Saatchi Art, and Artfinder
- Managing inventory and shipping logistics

Chapter 7: Selling Offline
- Approaching local galleries and art fairs
- Hosting open studio events and art parties
- Consignment agreements and commission sales

Chapter 8: Handling Sales Transactions
- Drafting contracts and invoices
- Accepting payments securely
- Providing certificates of authenticity

Chapter 9: Building Long-Term Relationships with Collectors
- Providing excellent customer service
- Maintaining communication with buyers
- Offering exclusive perks and incentives for repeat customers

Chapter 10: Legal and Ethical Considerations
- Copyright and intellectual property rights
- Licensing agreements and reproduction rights
- Ensuring transparency and honesty in your business practices

Chapter 11: Overcoming Challenges and Rejection
- Dealing with rejection and criticism
- Staying motivated during slow sales periods
- Seeking support from fellow artists and mentors

Chapter 12: Scaling Your Art Business
- Hiring assistants or interns
- Outsourcing tasks like marketing or shipping
- Expanding into new markets or product lines

Chapter 13: Financial Management for Artists
- Budgeting and managing cash flow
- Tracking expenses and income
- Investing in your art career wisely

Chapter 14: The Future of Selling Art
- Trends in the art market and industry
- Embracing technology and innovation
- Maintaining adaptability and resilience as an artistpreneur

Chapter 15: Continuous Learning and Growth
- Lifelong Learning in the Arts
- Strategies for Continuous Growth
- Embracing a Growth Mindset

Appendix: Resources for Artists
- List of recommended books, websites, and podcasts
- Templates for contracts, invoices, and marketing materials
- Directory of art supply stores, printing services, and professional organizations

Acknowledgments
- Thanking supporters, mentors, and collaborators who helped along the way

About the Author
- Brief biography and contact information for the author

Chapter 1: Introduction to Selling Your Art

Art is more than just a form of self-expression; it's a valuable commodity that holds the potential to enrich not only your life but also the lives of others. In this chapter, we'll embark on a journey to explore the intricate world of selling your original artwork. Whether you're a seasoned artist looking to expand your market reach or an emerging talent eager to turn your passion into profit, this guide will provide you with the knowledge and tools necessary to navigate the complex landscape of the art market.

Understanding the Market for Original Artwork

The art market is a dynamic and multifaceted arena where artists, collectors, galleries, and buyers converge to buy, sell, and trade original artwork. It encompasses a wide range of mediums, styles, and genres, from traditional paintings and sculptures to digital art and mixed media installations. Understanding the nuances of the art market is crucial for success as an artist entrepreneur.

- Market Trends: Stay informed about current trends and developments in the art world, such as emerging artists, popular styles, and collector preferences. Pay attention to shifts in consumer behavior and buying patterns.

- Market Segmentation: Recognize that the art market is diverse, with different segments catering to various tastes, budgets, and demographics. Identify your target audience and tailor your marketing strategies accordingly.

- Pricing Dynamics: Pricing your artwork appropriately requires a keen understanding of market dynamics, including factors such as the artist's reputation, the size and complexity of the piece, and prevailing market conditions. Conduct thorough research to ensure your prices are competitive yet reflective of the value of your work.

Identifying Your Target Audience

Knowing your audience is essential for effectively marketing and selling your artwork. Your target audience consists of individuals who are most likely to appreciate and purchase your art. By understanding their preferences, interests, and purchasing behaviors, you can tailor your artistic practice and promotional efforts to resonate with them.

- Demographic Factors: Consider demographic factors such as age, gender, income level, and geographic location when identifying your target audience. Certain demographics may be more inclined to collect art or invest in original pieces.

- Psychographic Profile: Delve deeper into the psychographic profile of your target audience by considering their lifestyles, values, interests, and motivations. What inspires them? What resonates with their personal tastes and aesthetic preferences?

- Market Segmentation: Segment your target audience based on common characteristics or behaviors, such as art collectors, interior designers, corporate clients, or art enthusiasts. Each segment may require a different approach in terms of marketing messaging and sales strategies.

Setting Realistic Goals and Expectations

As you embark on your journey to sell your original artwork, it's important to set realistic goals and expectations for yourself. While the prospect of achieving fame and fortune as an artist may be enticing, success in the art world often requires patience, persistence, and resilience.

- Define Your Objectives: Clarify your short-term and long-term goals as an artist entrepreneur. Do you aspire to gain recognition within your local art community, secure representation by a prestigious gallery, or achieve financial independence through art sales?

- Establish Milestones: Break down your goals into manageable milestones or benchmarks that you can work towards incrementally. Celebrate small victories along the way to stay motivated and focused on your journey.

- Manage Expectations: Acknowledge that the path to success in the art world may be fraught with challenges and setbacks. Not every artwork will sell immediately, and rejection is a natural part of the artistic process. Cultivate a mindset of resilience and perseverance to overcome obstacles and continue pursuing your passion for art.

In the chapters that follow, we'll delve deeper into the strategies and tactics you can employ to effectively market, promote, and sell your original artwork. By mastering the art of selling, you can not only achieve financial success but also share your creativity with the world and leave a lasting impact on those who experience your art.

Chapter 2: Building Your Brand as an Artist

Your brand is more than just a logo or a tagline; it's the essence of who you are as an artist and what you represent to the world. In this chapter, we'll explore the importance of building a strong and distinctive brand identity as a foundation for success in selling your original artwork.

Crafting Your Unique Artistic Identity

Your artistic identity is the core of your brand—it encompasses your style, themes, techniques, and creative vision. It's what sets you apart from other artists and makes your work recognizable and memorable to collectors and art enthusiasts.

- Self-Reflection: Take time to reflect on your artistic journey and identify the themes, motifs, and subjects that resonate most deeply with you. What inspires you? What messages or emotions do you seek to convey through your art?

- Developing Your Style: Experiment with different mediums, techniques, and approaches to find your unique artistic voice. Whether your style is bold and expressive or subtle and nuanced, strive to develop a cohesive body of work that reflects your personal aesthetic.

- Consistency and Authenticity: Consistency is key to building a strong brand identity. Aim for consistency in terms of style, quality, and message across your portfolio of artwork. Authenticity is equally important—stay true to yourself and your artistic vision, and avoid imitating others or conforming to trends for the sake of popularity.

Establishing an Online Presence

In today's digital age, an online presence is essential for artists seeking to reach a wider audience and connect with potential buyers around the world. Your website and social media profiles serve as virtual galleries where collectors and art enthusiasts can discover and engage with your artwork.

- Creating a Professional Website: Invest in a professionally designed website that showcases your artwork in a visually appealing and user-friendly manner. Include high-quality images of your artwork, a biography or artist statement, information about upcoming exhibitions or events, and contact details for inquiries and sales.

- Leveraging Social Media: Utilize social media platforms such as Instagram, Facebook, X (formerly Twitter), and Pinterest to share your artwork, engage with followers, and attract new audiences. Consistency is key—regularly post updates, behind-the-scenes glimpses of your creative process, and stories that resonate with your audience.

- Engaging with Your Audience: Foster meaningful connections with your online audience by responding to comments, messages, and inquiries promptly and authentically. Share insights into your artistic process, stories behind your artwork, and glimpses into your life as an artist to humanize your brand and build rapport with your followers.

Networking and Collaborating with Other Artists and Galleries

Networking and collaboration are invaluable tools for expanding your reach, gaining exposure, and forging meaningful connections within the art community. By building relationships with fellow artists, galleries, collectors, and industry professionals, you can open doors to new opportunities and elevate your artistic career.

- Joining Artist Communities: Seek out local art organizations, co-working spaces, and online communities where artists gather to share resources, support each other, and collaborate on projects. Participate in group exhibitions, workshops, and networking events to expand your circle of contacts and build relationships with peers.

- Building Relationships with Galleries: Research and approach galleries that align with your artistic style, values, and career goals. Prepare a professional portfolio of your artwork, including high-quality images, a biography, artist statement, and exhibition history, to present to gallery owners or curators. Be open to feedback and constructive criticism, and be proactive in following up on leads and opportunities.

- Collaborating with Other Creatives: Explore collaboration opportunities with artists from different disciplines, such as musicians, writers, photographers, or designers. Collaborative projects can spark creativity, broaden your audience reach, and introduce your artwork to new contexts and audiences.

By crafting a compelling brand identity, establishing a strong online presence, and nurturing relationships within the art community, you can position yourself for success as an artist entrepreneur. In the chapters that follow, we'll delve deeper into the strategies and tactics you can employ to market, promote, and sell your original artwork effectively in today's competitive art market.

Chapter 3: Creating Marketable Artwork

Creating artwork that resonates with buyers while staying true to your artistic vision is a delicate balance that all artists must navigate. In this chapter, we'll explore strategies for developing original artwork with commercial appeal without compromising your creative integrity.

Developing Your Artistic Style

Your artistic style is the hallmark of your work—it's what sets you apart from other artists and creates a unique visual identity that collectors and art enthusiasts can recognize and appreciate. Developing and refining your artistic style is a continuous process of exploration, experimentation, and self-discovery.

- Exploring Different Mediums and Techniques: Experiment with a variety of mediums, such as oil paint, acrylics, watercolors, pastels, or digital media, to discover which ones resonate most with your artistic sensibilities. Likewise, explore different techniques, styles, and approaches to art-making to find your own unique voice.

- Finding Inspiration: Draw inspiration from a diverse range of sources, including nature, literature, music, culture, history, and personal experiences. Keep a sketchbook or visual journal to capture ideas, sketches, and observations that inspire your creative process.

- Refining Your Vision: Continuously refine and evolve your artistic vision by pushing yourself outside of your comfort zone, embracing experimentation and risk-taking, and seeking feedback from peers, mentors, and trusted critics. Stay open-minded and receptive to new ideas and perspectives that challenge and inspire you.

Balancing Creativity with Commercial Appeal

While artistic freedom and self-expression are paramount, artists must also consider the commercial viability of their work when seeking to sell their artwork to a broader audience. Balancing creativity with commercial appeal requires a nuanced understanding of market trends, collector preferences, and the broader cultural landscape.

- Understanding Market Trends: Stay informed about current trends and developments in the art world, including popular styles, themes, and mediums. While it's important to stay true to your artistic vision, being aware of market trends can help you create artwork that resonates with contemporary audiences.

- Catering to Collector Preferences: Consider the preferences and tastes of your target audience when creating artwork for sale. Pay attention to feedback from collectors, galleries, and art advisors, and adapt your artistic practice accordingly to meet the demands of the market.

- Maintaining Authenticity: While it's important to create artwork with commercial appeal, authenticity should always be your guiding principle. Avoid chasing trends or compromising your artistic integrity for the sake of popularity or profit. Instead, focus on creating artwork that reflects your unique perspective, voice, and vision.

Leveraging Your Unique Selling Points

As an artist, you possess a unique set of skills, experiences, and perspectives that set you apart from other creators. Leveraging your unique selling points—whether it's your distinctive style, technical expertise, or personal story—can help you stand out in a crowded marketplace and attract buyers to your artwork.

- Identifying Your USP: Take stock of your strengths, talents, and accomplishments as an artist, and identify what sets you apart from your peers. Do you have a signature technique or aesthetic? A compelling personal narrative or background? A track record of awards, exhibitions, or accolades? Highlighting these unique selling points can help you differentiate yourself and your artwork from the competition.

- Communicating Your Brand Story: Craft a compelling brand story that communicates who you are as an artist, what inspires you, and why your artwork matters. Share insights into your creative process, sources of inspiration, and the meaning behind your work to engage and connect with potential buyers on a deeper level.

- Building Trust and Credibility: Establishing trust and credibility with collectors is essential for building long-term relationships and securing repeat sales. Be transparent and authentic in your interactions with buyers, deliver high-quality artwork and customer service, and stand behind your work with confidence and pride.

By developing a strong artistic style, balancing creativity with commercial appeal, and leveraging your unique selling points, you can create artwork that resonates with buyers and commands attention in the competitive art market. In the chapters that follow, we'll delve deeper into the strategies and tactics you can employ to effectively market, promote, and sell your original artwork to a global audience of collectors and enthusiasts.

Chapter 4: Pricing Your Artwork

Determining the right price for your artwork is a crucial aspect of selling your original pieces. Pricing too high may deter potential buyers, while pricing too low may undermine the value of your work and your credibility as an artist. In this chapter, we'll explore the factors to consider when pricing your artwork and strategies for pricing it competitively.

Factors to Consider When Pricing Your Art

Pricing artwork is not a one-size-fits-all endeavor—it requires careful consideration of various factors that contribute to the value and desirability of your pieces. By understanding these factors, you can establish prices that reflect the worth of your artwork and resonate with potential buyers.

- Artistic Merit: Evaluate the artistic merit of your artwork based on criteria such as creativity, technical skill, originality, and conceptual depth. Consider how your work compares to that of other artists in terms of quality and innovation.

- Size and Complexity: Larger or more intricate pieces typically command higher prices due to the increased time, materials, and effort required to create them. Take into account the size, scale, and complexity of each artwork when determining its price.

- Materials and Production Costs: Factor in the cost of materials, supplies, and production expenses when pricing your artwork. Consider the quality of materials used, as well as any specialized techniques or processes involved in creating the piece.

- Artist Reputation and Track Record: Your reputation as an artist and your track record of exhibitions, awards, and sales can influence the perceived value of your artwork. As your reputation grows, you may be able to command higher prices for your work.

- Market Demand and Trends: Assess the demand for your artwork within the market and consider prevailing trends and preferences among collectors. Factors such as popularity, scarcity, and relevance to current artistic movements can impact the perceived value of your work.

Strategies for Pricing Your Art Competitively

Pricing your artwork competitively requires a balance between maximizing your earning potential and ensuring that your prices are fair and reasonable for buyers. By employing strategic pricing strategies, you can position your artwork effectively within the market while maintaining its perceived value.

- Research Comparable Artworks: Research the prices of comparable artworks by other artists with similar styles, mediums, and levels of recognition. This can provide valuable insights into pricing trends and benchmarks within your niche.

- Calculate Costs and Expenses: Calculate the total costs and expenses associated with creating each artwork, including materials, labor, studio rent, marketing, and overhead expenses. Use this information as a baseline for determining your pricing structure.

- Factor in Your Time and Expertise: Don't overlook the value of your time and expertise as an artist. Consider how much time you invest in creating each piece, as well as the years of experience, training, and skill development that contribute to your artistic practice.

- Consider Pricing Tiers: Consider offering artworks at different price points to accommodate buyers with varying budgets. This can include smaller works or limited-edition prints at lower price points, as well as larger, more elaborate pieces at higher price points.

- Be Transparent and Consistent: Be transparent about your pricing methodology and ensure consistency in your pricing across different sales channels and venues. Avoid arbitrary discounts or price fluctuations that may confuse or alienate potential buyers.

Negotiating Sales and Discounts

While establishing clear pricing guidelines is important, flexibility in negotiating sales and offering discounts can help facilitate transactions and cultivate goodwill with buyers. When negotiating sales or offering discounts, consider the following strategies:

- Set a Minimum Acceptable Price: Determine the lowest price at which you are willing to sell each artwork, taking into account your costs, expenses, and desired profit margin. Use this as a starting point for negotiations with potential buyers.

- Offer Incentives for Multiple Purchases: Encourage buyers to purchase multiple artworks by offering discounts or incentives for bulk purchases. This can help increase your sales volume and cultivate repeat business from collectors.

- Provide Value-Added Services: Enhance the perceived value of your artwork by offering value-added services such as custom framing, installation assistance, or personalized certificates of authenticity. These added benefits can justify higher prices and make your artwork more attractive to buyers.

- Be Flexible and Open-Minded: Be willing to negotiate with potential buyers and consider their individual needs and preferences. While it's important to maintain the integrity of your pricing structure, being flexible and open-minded can help facilitate mutually beneficial transactions.

By carefully considering the various factors that contribute to the value of your artwork and employing strategic pricing strategies, you can establish prices that reflect the worth of your work and resonate with potential buyers. In the chapters that follow, we'll delve deeper into the strategies and tactics you can employ to effectively market, promote, and sell your original artwork to a global audience of collectors and enthusiasts.

Chapter 5: Marketing and Promotion

In the competitive world of art sales, effective marketing and promotion are essential for getting your artwork noticed, building your brand, and attracting potential buyers. This chapter explores various strategies and tactics you can use to market and promote your original artwork to a wider audience.

Utilizing Social Media Platforms Effectively

Social media platforms have revolutionized the way artists connect with their audience and promote their artwork. With billions of users worldwide, platforms like Instagram, Facebook, Twitter, and Pinterest offer powerful tools for showcasing your art, engaging with followers, and attracting new fans and collectors.

- Visual Storytelling: Use the visual nature of social media to tell compelling stories about your artwork, your creative process, and the inspiration behind your pieces. Share high-quality images, videos, and behind-the-scenes glimpses that resonate with your audience and invite them into your world as an artist.

- Consistent Branding: Maintain a consistent brand identity across all your social media profiles, including your profile picture, bio, and content style. Use cohesive visual elements such as colors, fonts, and logos to create a unified and recognizable brand presence that reflects your artistic identity.

- Engagement and Interaction: Foster meaningful connections with your audience by actively engaging with followers through likes, comments, and direct messages. Respond promptly to inquiries, acknowledge feedback, and show appreciation for support from your fans and collectors.

- Hashtag Strategy: Harness the power of hashtags to expand the reach of your posts and attract new followers who are interested in art. Use relevant and trending hashtags related to your artwork, artistic style, medium, and themes to increase visibility and discoverability on social media.

Building an Email List and Newsletter

Email marketing remains one of the most effective tools for reaching your audience directly and nurturing relationships with potential buyers over time. Building an email list allows you to communicate directly with subscribers, share updates and announcements, and promote your artwork to a targeted audience.

- Offer Incentives to Subscribe: Encourage visitors to your website or social media profiles to subscribe to your email list by offering incentives such as exclusive discounts, access to VIP events or previews, or free downloadable content such as ebooks or digital artwork.

- Segment Your Email List: Segment your email list based on factors such as purchase history, engagement level, and interests to deliver more personalized and relevant content to subscribers. Tailor your email campaigns to specific segments of your audience to maximize engagement and conversion rates.

- Provide Value-Added Content: Keep subscribers engaged and interested by providing value-added content in your email newsletters, such as artist interviews, studio updates, behind-the-scenes stories, and tips for collecting and appreciating art.

- Call to Action: Include clear and compelling calls to action in your email newsletters to encourage subscribers to take the next step, whether it's visiting your online store, attending an upcoming exhibition or event, or contacting you for commissions or inquiries.

Leveraging Art Shows, Exhibitions, and Galleries

Participating in art shows, exhibitions, and galleries is a time-honored tradition for artists seeking to showcase their work, connect with collectors, and establish credibility within the art community. Whether online or offline, these events offer valuable opportunities to gain exposure and generate sales.

- Research Opportunities: Research and identify art shows, exhibitions, and galleries that align with your artistic style, target audience, and career goals. Look for opportunities to participate in juried shows, group exhibitions, solo shows, art fairs, and gallery representation.

- Prepare Your Portfolio: Prepare a professional portfolio of your artwork, including high-quality images, artist statement, biography, and exhibition history, to submit to curators, jurors, and gallery owners. Tailor your portfolio to each opportunity and showcase your strongest and most relevant pieces.

- Network and Build Relationships: Attend art shows, openings, receptions, and networking events to connect with fellow artists, collectors, curators, and gallery owners. Build genuine relationships with industry professionals and seek opportunities for collaboration, representation, and exposure.

- Follow Up: Follow up with contacts you meet at art shows and exhibitions to thank them for their time and express your interest in future collaborations or opportunities. Stay connected with collectors and gallery owners by sending updates about new artwork, upcoming events, and recent achievements.

By utilizing social media platforms effectively, building an email list and newsletter, and leveraging art shows, exhibitions, and galleries, you can expand your reach, attract new collectors, and promote your artwork to a wider audience. In the chapters that follow, we'll delve deeper into the strategies and tactics you can employ to effectively market, promote, and sell your original artwork in today's competitive art market.

Chapter 6: Selling Online

The internet has revolutionized the way artists sell their artwork, providing access to a global audience of collectors and enthusiasts. In this chapter, we'll explore the strategies and best practices for selling your original artwork online, from setting up an e-commerce website to leveraging online marketplaces.

Setting Up an E-commerce Website

An e-commerce website serves as your online storefront, allowing you to showcase your artwork, manage sales transactions, and connect directly with buyers. Setting up an e-commerce website gives you greater control over your sales process and branding, and provides a platform for building relationships with customers.

- Choose a Platform: Select an e-commerce platform that meets your needs and budget, such as Shopify, Squarespace, WooCommerce, or BigCommerce. Consider factors such as ease of use, customization options, payment processing fees, and integration with other tools and services.

- Design Your Website: Design a visually appealing and user-friendly website that highlights your artwork and reflects your brand identity. Use high-quality images, clear navigation, and compelling copy to engage visitors and encourage them to explore your portfolio and make purchases.

- Optimize for Search Engines: Optimize your website for search engines (SEO) to improve its visibility and ranking in search results. Use relevant keywords, meta tags, and descriptions throughout your site to help potential buyers find your artwork when searching online.

- Implement Secure Payment Processing: Choose a secure payment gateway to process transactions securely and protect sensitive customer information. Offer multiple payment options, such as credit cards, PayPal, and other digital wallets, to accommodate different buyer preferences.

Utilizing Online Marketplaces

Online marketplaces provide artists with additional opportunities to reach a broader audience and sell their artwork alongside other artists and creators. Whether you're selling prints, originals, or custom commissions, leveraging online marketplaces can expand your reach and increase your sales potential.

- Etsy: Etsy is a popular online marketplace for handmade and vintage goods, including artwork, crafts, and jewelry. Create a seller account and set up a shop to list your artwork, manage orders, and connect with buyers around the world.

- Saatchi Art: Saatchi Art is an online platform that connects artists with collectors, galleries, and art enthusiasts. Apply to become a Saatchi Art artist and upload your artwork to showcase and sell to a global audience.

- Artfinder: Artfinder is an online marketplace that specializes in contemporary art, offering a curated selection of paintings, sculptures, prints, and photography. Join Artfinder as an artist and list your artwork for sale to a community of collectors and buyers.

- Society6, Redbubble, and Printful: These print-on-demand platforms allow artists to sell their artwork on a variety of products, including prints, posters, apparel, home decor, and accessories. Upload your designs and earn royalties on each sale without the hassle of inventory management or fulfillment.

Managing Inventory and Shipping Logistics

Effective inventory management and shipping logistics are essential for ensuring a smooth and seamless online selling experience for both you and your customers. By implementing efficient processes and tools, you can streamline order fulfillment, minimize errors, and provide a positive buying experience.

- Inventory Management: Keep track of your inventory levels and update your online listings regularly to reflect available artwork. Use inventory management software or spreadsheets to track sales, monitor stock levels, and reorder supplies as needed.

- Packaging and Shipping: Invest in high-quality packaging materials to protect your artwork during transit and ensure it arrives in pristine condition. Calculate shipping costs accurately based on factors such as size, weight, and destination, and offer multiple shipping options to accommodate different buyer preferences.

- Shipping Policies and Terms: Clearly communicate your shipping policies, terms, and estimated delivery times on your website and product listings. Provide tracking information and shipping updates to keep customers informed throughout the shipping process.

- International Sales: Consider expanding your sales reach to international buyers by offering international shipping options and providing information about customs duties, taxes, and import regulations. Use international shipping carriers and services to ensure reliable and cost-effective delivery to customers worldwide.

By setting up an e-commerce website, utilizing online marketplaces, and effectively managing inventory and shipping logistics, you can maximize your online sales potential and reach a global audience of collectors and enthusiasts. In the chapters that follow, we'll delve deeper into the strategies and tactics you can employ to effectively market, promote, and sell your original artwork in today's competitive online marketplace.

Chapter 7: Selling Offline

While the digital landscape offers tremendous opportunities for selling artwork online, offline channels remain an important avenue for reaching collectors and engaging with art enthusiasts in person. In this chapter, we'll explore various strategies for selling your original artwork offline, including approaching local galleries, participating in art fairs, and hosting open studio events.

Approaching Local Galleries

Local galleries serve as gateways to the local art scene and can provide valuable exposure and opportunities for artists to showcase their work to a captive audience of collectors and art enthusiasts. Approaching local galleries requires research, preparation, and a professional presentation of your artwork.

- Research: Research local galleries in your area and familiarize yourself with their curatorial focus, aesthetic preferences, and submission guidelines. Visit galleries in person to get a sense of their exhibition spaces, clientele, and the types of artwork they represent.

- Prepare Your Portfolio: Prepare a professional portfolio of your artwork, including high-quality images, an artist statement, biography, and exhibition history. Tailor your portfolio to each gallery's aesthetic and thematic focus, and highlight pieces that align with their programming.

- Submitting Your Work: Follow each gallery's submission guidelines carefully when submitting your artwork for consideration. Submit digital images of your artwork along with a cover letter or artist statement introducing yourself and explaining why you believe your work would be a good fit for their gallery.

- Follow Up: Follow up with galleries after submitting your work to inquire about the status of your submission and express your continued interest in exhibiting with them. Be persistent but respectful, and be prepared to handle rejection gracefully while continuing to explore other opportunities.

Participating in Art Fairs and Exhibitions

Art fairs and exhibitions offer artists a platform to showcase their work to a broader audience of collectors, curators, and art enthusiasts in a dynamic and immersive setting. Participating in art fairs and exhibitions requires planning, preparation, and effective presentation of your artwork.

- Research: Research upcoming art fairs, exhibitions, and events in your region or within your niche, and identify opportunities that align with your artistic style, goals, and target audience. Consider factors such as the reputation of the event, the caliber of participating artists, and the expected attendance.

- Apply for Participation: Apply for participation in art fairs and exhibitions by submitting an application along with images of your artwork, an artist statement, biography, and exhibition history. Pay attention to application deadlines and requirements, and provide all requested information and materials.

- Prepare Your Booth or Exhibition Space: Prepare your booth or exhibition space with careful attention to detail, considering factors such as lighting, display racks or pedestals, signage, and promotional materials. Create an inviting and visually appealing presentation that highlights your artwork and draws visitors in.

- Engage with Visitors: Engage with visitors to your booth or exhibition space by welcoming them, answering questions about your artwork, and sharing insights into your creative process and inspiration. Collect contact information from interested buyers and follow up after the event to nurture relationships and facilitate sales.

Hosting Open Studio Events and Art Parties

Hosting open studio events and art parties provides artists with a unique opportunity to connect directly with collectors and art enthusiasts in an intimate and informal setting. By inviting guests into your studio or home, you can showcase your artwork, share your creative process, and foster meaningful connections with potential buyers.

- Plan Your Event: Plan your open studio event or art party carefully, considering factors such as date, time, location, and guest list. Promote your event through social media, email newsletters, and word-of-mouth invitations to attract attendees and generate buzz.

- Prepare Your Space: Prepare your studio or home for the event by cleaning and organizing your workspace, setting up displays of your artwork, and creating a welcoming atmosphere for guests. Provide refreshments, music, and entertainment to enhance the experience for attendees.

- Interact with Guests: Interact with guests during the event by welcoming them, offering guided tours of your studio or home, and engaging in conversations about your artwork. Be approachable, enthusiastic, and knowledgeable about your work, and be prepared to answer questions and provide insights.

- Facilitate Sales: Facilitate sales during the event by offering special promotions, discounts, or incentives for attendees to purchase artwork. Provide pricing information and payment options, and be prepared to handle sales transactions on-site or follow up with interested buyers after the event.

By approaching local galleries, participating in art fairs and exhibitions, and hosting open studio events and art parties, you can expand your offline sales channels, reach new audiences, and establish connections with collectors and art enthusiasts in your community and beyond. In the chapters that follow, we'll delve deeper into the strategies and tactics you can employ to effectively market, promote, and sell your original artwork through a combination of online and offline channels.

Chapter 8: Handling Sales Transactions

Effectively managing sales transactions is essential for ensuring a smooth and seamless experience for both you and your customers. In this chapter, we'll explore the various aspects of handling sales transactions, from drafting contracts and invoices to accepting payments securely and providing certificates of authenticity.

Drafting Contracts and Invoices

Contracts and invoices serve as legal documents that outline the terms and conditions of a sale, including pricing, payment terms, delivery arrangements, and any additional terms or provisions. Drafting clear and comprehensive contracts and invoices is essential for protecting your rights as an artist and ensuring that both parties understand their obligations.

- Contract Essentials: Include essential elements in your sales contracts, such as a description of the artwork being sold, the purchase price, payment terms (including any deposits or installment payments), delivery arrangements, and provisions for disputes or cancellations. Consider consulting with a legal professional to ensure that your contracts comply with relevant laws and regulations.

- Invoice Details: Include detailed information in your invoices, such as the buyer's name and contact information, a description of the artwork purchased, the purchase price, any applicable taxes or fees, and payment instructions. Provide clear instructions for payment methods and deadlines to facilitate timely payment.

- Terms and Conditions: Clearly outline the terms and conditions of the sale in your contracts and invoices, including policies related to returns, exchanges, refunds, and damages. Specify any warranties or guarantees offered with the artwork, as well as any restrictions on reproduction or resale.

Accepting Payments Securely

Accepting payments securely is crucial for protecting sensitive financial information and preventing fraud or unauthorized transactions. Whether selling artwork online or offline, it's important to offer multiple payment options and ensure that transactions are processed safely and securely.

- Online Payment Gateways: Choose a secure online payment gateway to process transactions securely on your e-commerce website or online marketplace. Use reputable payment processors such as PayPal, Stripe, or Square, which offer advanced security features such as encryption, fraud detection, and PCI compliance.

- Offline Payment Methods: Accept offline payment methods such as cash, checks, or bank transfers for in-person sales or transactions conducted outside of your e-commerce website. Provide clear instructions for payment instructions and ensure that funds are received and verified before releasing the artwork to the buyer.

- Payment Processing Fees: Be aware of any fees associated with processing payments, such as transaction fees, currency conversion fees, or processing fees charged by payment processors. Factor these fees into your pricing structure or pass them on to the buyer as a separate charge.

Providing Certificates of Authenticity

A certificate of authenticity (COA) is a document that provides evidence of the authenticity and provenance of an artwork, including details such as the artist's name, title of the artwork, medium, dimensions, date of creation, and signature. Providing COAs with your artwork adds credibility and value for collectors and enhances the perceived value of your work.

- Creating COAs: Create professional-looking certificates of authenticity for each artwork you sell, either using templates or custom designs. Include essential information about the artwork, such as its title, medium, dimensions, date of creation, and a brief description of the piece.

- Sign and Number: Sign and number each certificate of authenticity to authenticate its validity and establish its uniqueness. Consider using a secure method of numbering, such as sequential numbering or holographic stickers, to prevent duplication or counterfeiting.

- Include Documentation: Include additional documentation with your COAs, such as receipts, invoices, or provenance records, to further authenticate the artwork and provide additional information for collectors. Maintain detailed records of sales and transactions for your own records and future reference.

By drafting clear and comprehensive contracts and invoices, accepting payments securely, and providing certificates of authenticity with your artwork, you can ensure a professional and transparent sales process that instills confidence in buyers and protects your rights as an artist. In the chapters that follow, we'll delve deeper into the strategies and tactics you can employ to effectively market, promote, and sell your original artwork in today's competitive art market.

Chapter 9: Building Long-Term Relationships with Collectors

Exceptional customer service is the cornerstone of a successful art business. By prioritizing the needs and satisfaction of your customers, you can build strong relationships, foster loyalty, and encourage repeat purchases. In this chapter, we'll explore strategies for providing exceptional customer service throughout the sales process and beyond.

Communicating Promptly and Professionally

Effective communication is key to providing exceptional customer service. Whether responding to inquiries, addressing concerns, or providing updates on orders, it's essential to communicate promptly, courteously, and professionally with your customers.

- Timely Responses: Respond to customer inquiries, messages, and emails in a timely manner, ideally within 24 to 48 hours. Acknowledge receipt of their communication, address their questions or concerns, and provide any necessary information or assistance promptly.

- Clear and Concise: Be clear and concise in your communications with customers, avoiding jargon or technical language that may be confusing. Use plain language and provide information in a straightforward manner to ensure that customers understand the information you're conveying.

- Professional Tone: Maintain a professional tone and demeanor in all your communications with customers, whether online, over the phone, or in person. Be courteous, respectful, and empathetic, and strive to exceed their expectations with your level of service.

Assisting with Purchase Decisions

As an artist, you play a crucial role in helping customers navigate the process of purchasing artwork. By offering personalized assistance, guidance, and recommendations, you can help customers make informed decisions and find artwork that resonates with them.

- Understand Customer Needs: Take the time to understand your customers' preferences, tastes, and budget constraints. Ask questions to clarify their needs and preferences, and offer personalized recommendations based on their interests and aesthetic preferences.

- Provide Information: Provide customers with detailed information about your artwork, including its inspiration, materials, dimensions, and pricing. Offer insights into your creative process, the meaning behind your work, and any special features or qualities that set it apart.

- Offer Options: Offer customers a range of options to choose from, including different sizes, mediums, and styles of artwork. Present complementary pieces or suggest additional artworks that may complement their existing collection or decor.

Handling Inquiries and Resolving Issues

Dealing with inquiries and resolving issues promptly and effectively is essential for maintaining customer satisfaction and loyalty. Whether addressing shipping delays, damaged artwork, or other concerns, it's important to respond promptly and take proactive steps to resolve the issue to the customer's satisfaction.

- Listen Actively: Listen actively to customers' concerns and feedback, allowing them to express their thoughts and feelings without interruption. Show empathy and understanding, and acknowledge their concerns before offering solutions or assistance.

- Take Ownership: Take ownership of any issues or problems that arise and take proactive steps to address them promptly. Apologize for any inconvenience or dissatisfaction experienced by the customer, and demonstrate your commitment to resolving the issue to their satisfaction.

- Offer Solutions: Offer solutions or alternatives to resolve the customer's issue, whether it's arranging for a replacement artwork, issuing a refund or credit, or providing additional compensation or incentives. Communicate transparently with the customer throughout the resolution process, keeping them informed of progress and next steps.

Following Up After the Sale

Following up with customers after the sale is an important part of providing exceptional customer service and building long-term relationships. By expressing gratitude, soliciting feedback, and staying connected, you can foster loyalty and encourage repeat purchases from satisfied customers.

- Express Gratitude: Express gratitude to customers for their purchase and support, whether through a personalized thank-you note, email, or phone call. Show appreciation for their business and for choosing to invest in your artwork.

- Solicit Feedback: Solicit feedback from customers about their purchasing experience, including what they liked and any areas for improvement. Use this feedback to identify strengths and weaknesses in your sales process and make adjustments to enhance the customer experience.

- Stay Connected: Stay connected with customers after the sale by keeping them informed of new artwork releases, upcoming events, or special promotions. Maintain an active presence on social media, email newsletters, or other channels to stay top of mind and encourage repeat purchases.

By prioritizing effective communication, assisting with purchase decisions, handling inquiries and resolving issues promptly, and following up after the sale, you can provide exceptional customer service that delights your customers and sets you apart from the competition. In the chapters that follow, we'll delve deeper into the strategies and tactics you can employ to effectively market, promote, and sell your original artwork in today's competitive art market.

Chapter 10: Legal and Ethical Considerations in Art Sales

Navigating the legal and ethical landscape of art sales is essential for artists seeking to protect their rights, maintain integrity, and build trust with collectors and buyers. In this chapter, we'll explore key legal and ethical considerations that artists should be aware of when selling their original artwork.

Copyright and Intellectual Property Rights

Copyright law protects artists' original works of authorship, including paintings, sculptures, drawings, and photographs, from unauthorized use or reproduction. Understanding copyright law is crucial for artists to protect their intellectual property rights and prevent infringement.

- Copyright Ownership: Artists automatically own the copyright to their original artwork as soon as it is created, granting them exclusive rights to reproduce, distribute, and display their work. Artists can further protect their rights by registering their artwork with the U.S. Copyright Office.

- Licensing and Permissions: Artists may choose to license their artwork to third parties for reproduction, distribution, or use in derivative works. It's important for artists to establish clear licensing agreements outlining the terms and conditions of use to protect their rights and ensure fair compensation.

- Fair Use and Derivative Works: Artists should be aware of the concept of fair use, which allows limited use of copyrighted material without permission for purposes such as criticism, commentary, or education. Artists should also exercise caution when creating derivative works based on existing copyrighted material to avoid infringement.

Authenticity and Provenance

Maintaining authenticity and provenance is essential for artists to establish the legitimacy and value of their artwork and build trust with collectors and buyers.

- Certificate of Authenticity: Artists should provide a certificate of authenticity with each artwork sold, verifying its origin, authenticity, and provenance. The certificate should include details such as the artist's name, title of the artwork, medium, dimensions, date of creation, and signature.

- Provenance Documentation: Artists should maintain detailed records of the history and ownership of their artwork, known as provenance documentation. Provenance documentation provides a record of the artwork's exhibition history, previous owners, and any relevant documentation or correspondence related to its creation and sale.

- Transparency and Disclosure: Artists should be transparent about the materials, techniques, and processes used in the creation of their artwork. Providing accurate and honest information to collectors and buyers fosters trust and confidence in the artist and the authenticity of their work.

Ethical Sales Practices

Maintaining ethical sales practices is essential for artists to uphold their reputation, integrity, and credibility in the art market.

- Pricing Transparency: Artists should be transparent about their pricing practices, ensuring that prices are fair, consistent, and reflective of the quality and value of their artwork. Avoiding price manipulation or deceptive pricing tactics is essential for maintaining trust with collectors and buyers.

- Representation and Disclosure: Artists should accurately represent their artwork in marketing materials, descriptions, and communications with collectors and buyers. Disclose any relevant information about the artwork, including its condition, provenance, and any restoration or repairs that have been made.

- Professional Conduct: Artists should conduct themselves professionally in all interactions with collectors, buyers, galleries, and industry professionals. Honesty, integrity, and respect for others are fundamental principles that should guide artists' behavior and relationships within the art community.

By understanding and adhering to legal and ethical considerations in art sales, artists can protect their rights, maintain integrity, and build trust with collectors and buyers, fostering long-term success and sustainability in their artistic careers.

Chapter 11: Overcoming Challenges and Rejection in Art Sales

In the journey of selling original artwork, artists often encounter challenges and face rejection. Learning to navigate these obstacles with resilience and determination is essential for maintaining motivation and achieving success. In this chapter, we'll explore common challenges artists may encounter in art sales and strategies for overcoming rejection and adversity.

Understanding Common Challenges

Artists may encounter various challenges when selling their original artwork, ranging from market fluctuations and competition to self-doubt and rejection. By understanding these challenges, artists can better prepare themselves and develop strategies for overcoming obstacles along the way.

- Market Fluctuations: The art market can be unpredictable, with trends shifting, demand fluctuating, and economic factors impacting sales. Artists may face challenges in navigating market fluctuations and adapting their sales strategies accordingly.

- Competition: The art world is highly competitive, with countless artists vying for attention and recognition. Artists may encounter challenges in standing out from the crowd and distinguishing their work in a crowded marketplace.

- Self-Doubt: Artists may experience self-doubt and uncertainty about the value and quality of their artwork, leading to feelings of inadequacy or imposter syndrome. Overcoming self-doubt is essential for artists to confidently promote and sell their work.

- Rejection: Rejection is a common experience for artists, whether it's rejection from galleries, exhibitions, or potential buyers. Dealing with rejection can be disheartening, but it's essential for artists to persevere and learn from setbacks.

Strategies for Overcoming Rejection

While rejection is inevitable in the art world, how artists respond to rejection can greatly impact their success and resilience. Here are some strategies for overcoming rejection and maintaining motivation in the face of adversity:

- Develop Resilience: Cultivate resilience by viewing rejection as a natural part of the artistic journey rather than a reflection of your worth or talent as an artist. Recognize that every rejection is an opportunity for growth and learning.

- Seek Feedback: Instead of dwelling on rejection, seek feedback from trusted mentors, peers, or industry professionals. Constructive criticism can provide valuable insights into areas for improvement and help you refine your artistic practice.

- Learn from Rejection: Use rejection as an opportunity to reflect on your goals, strategies, and approach to selling your artwork. Identify areas where you can make adjustments or improvements, whether it's refining your portfolio, expanding your network, or enhancing your marketing efforts.

- Stay Positive and Persistent: Maintain a positive outlook and stay persistent in pursuing your goals, even in the face of setbacks and challenges. Focus on the aspects of your art practice that bring you joy and fulfillment, and remain committed to your artistic vision.

Finding Support and Community

Building a strong support network and community of fellow artists can provide invaluable encouragement, guidance, and camaraderie in times of challenge and rejection. Seek out opportunities to connect with other artists, whether through local art groups, online forums, or social media communities.

- Share Experiences: Share your experiences, challenges, and successes with fellow artists who can relate to your journey. By sharing openly and honestly, you can find support, encouragement, and solidarity within the art community.

- Offer Support: Offer support and encouragement to other artists facing similar challenges. Building a supportive community where artists lift each other up can foster a sense of belonging and resilience in the face of rejection.

- Celebrate Small Wins: Celebrate your achievements, no matter how small, and acknowledge the progress you've made on your artistic journey. Recognize that success in art sales is often gradual and incremental, and every step forward is worth celebrating.

By understanding common challenges, developing resilience, seeking feedback, and finding support within the art community, artists can overcome rejection and adversity and continue to pursue their passion for creating and selling original artwork. Remember that rejection is not a reflection of your talent or worth as an artist, but rather an opportunity for growth and self-discovery on your artistic journey.

Chapter 12: Scaling Your Art Business

Scaling your art business involves expanding your reach, increasing your sales volume, and growing your brand to achieve greater success and sustainability. In this chapter, we'll explore strategies for scaling your art business effectively, from expanding your product offerings and diversifying your revenue streams to leveraging technology and building strategic partnerships.

Expanding Your Product Offerings

One of the key strategies for scaling your art business is to expand your product offerings beyond original artwork. By diversifying your product line, you can appeal to a broader audience and generate additional revenue streams.

- Prints and Reproductions: Offer prints, posters, and limited edition reproductions of your original artwork to make your art more accessible to a wider audience. Consider partnering with a print-on-demand service or local printer to produce high-quality reproductions of your artwork.

- Merchandise and Lifestyle Products: Explore opportunities to create merchandise and lifestyle products featuring your artwork, such as apparel, accessories, home decor, and stationery. Collaborate with manufacturers or use print-on-demand services to produce custom products that showcase your unique artistic style.

- Commissions and Custom Work: Offer commission-based services and custom artwork to cater to clients' specific preferences and needs. Consider offering personalized portraits, custom illustrations, or bespoke artwork tailored to individual clients or businesses.

Diversifying Your Revenue Streams

Diversifying your revenue streams is essential for building a sustainable art business and reducing reliance on any single source of income. By exploring multiple revenue streams, you can mitigate risk and maximize your earning potential as an artist.

- Online Sales Platforms: Expand your presence on online sales platforms and art marketplaces to reach a broader audience and increase your sales volume. Consider selling your artwork on multiple platforms, including your own website, online galleries, and social media channels.

- Licensing and Collaboration: Explore opportunities to license your artwork for use in various commercial applications, such as advertising, publishing, and product packaging. Partner with brands, companies, or licensing agencies to explore collaborative opportunities and expand your reach into new markets.

- Teaching and Workshops: Share your expertise and skills with others by offering art classes, workshops, or online courses. Teach painting techniques, drawing fundamentals, or specialized skills to aspiring artists and enthusiasts, generating additional income while sharing your passion for art.

Leveraging Technology and Automation

Technology can be a powerful tool for scaling your art business and streamlining your operations. By leveraging technology and automation, you can save time, reduce administrative tasks, and focus more on creating and selling your artwork.

- E-Commerce Platforms: Invest in an e-commerce platform or website builder to create a professional online store for selling your artwork directly to customers. Choose a platform that offers features such as secure payment processing, inventory management, and customizable storefronts.

- Email Marketing and Automation: Build and nurture relationships with your audience through email marketing and automation. Use email marketing software to send targeted campaigns, newsletters, and promotional offers to your subscribers, keeping them engaged and informed about your latest artwork and offerings.

- Art Management Software: Consider using art management software or platforms designed specifically for artists to organize and streamline your art business operations. These tools can help you manage inventory, track sales, create invoices, and analyze performance metrics, allowing you to focus more on creating art and growing your business.

Building Strategic Partnerships

Collaborating with strategic partners can help you expand your reach, access new markets, and grow your art business more effectively. Look for opportunities to build mutually beneficial partnerships with galleries, retailers, brands, and other artists.

- Gallery Representation: Partner with galleries or art consultants to exhibit and sell your artwork in physical gallery spaces. Gallery representation can provide exposure to collectors, curators, and art enthusiasts, helping you reach a broader audience and establish your credibility as an artist.

- Retail Partnerships: Collaborate with retailers, boutiques, or online marketplaces to sell your artwork through third-party channels. Partnering with retailers can help you reach new customers and expand your distribution network, while also providing retailers with unique and compelling products to offer their customers.

- Cross-Promotion and Collaborations: Explore opportunities for cross-promotion and collaborations with other artists, brands, or influencers in complementary industries. Collaborative projects, joint exhibitions, or co-branded products can help you reach new audiences and leverage the existing fan bases and networks of your partners.

By expanding your product offerings, diversifying your revenue streams, leveraging technology and automation, and building strategic partnerships, you can scale your art business and achieve greater success as an artist. Remember to stay flexible, adapt to changes in the market, and continue to innovate and evolve your business model to meet the needs of your audience and grow your brand in the long term.

Chapter 13: Financial Management for Artists

Effective financial management is essential for artists to sustain their artistic practice, support their livelihood, and achieve long-term success in the art business. In this chapter, we'll explore key financial principles and strategies to help artists manage their finances responsibly and achieve their financial goals.

Budgeting and Planning

Creating a budget and financial plan is the foundation of sound financial management for artists. By establishing a budget, artists can track their income and expenses, allocate resources effectively, and make informed decisions about their finances.

- Income Sources: Identify all sources of income as an artist, including sales of artwork, commissions, grants, teaching opportunities, and other sources of revenue. Calculate your total monthly and annual income to understand your earning potential.

- Expenses: Track your expenses carefully, including art supplies, studio rent, marketing and promotion costs, website hosting fees, and other business expenses. Categorize your expenses to understand where your money is being spent and identify areas for potential savings or optimization.

- Savings and Investments: Set aside a portion of your income for savings and investments to build financial security and prepare for future expenses or emergencies. Consider opening a dedicated savings account or investment account to help your money grow over time.

Pricing and Pricing Strategy

Setting the right prices for your artwork is crucial for ensuring that your work is valued appropriately and that you can sustain your artistic practice financially. Develop a pricing strategy that takes into account factors such as the cost of materials, time spent on creating artwork, market demand, and your reputation as an artist.

- Cost of Materials: Calculate the cost of materials used to create each artwork, including canvas, paint, brushes, and other supplies. Factor in the cost of framing, packaging, and shipping for additional expenses associated with selling artwork.

- Time and Labor: Consider the time and labor involved in creating each artwork when setting prices. Estimate the number of hours spent on sketching, painting, and finishing each piece to determine a fair hourly rate for your time and expertise.

- Market Research: Research the prices of comparable artwork by other artists in your niche or style to understand market trends and pricing benchmarks. Consider factors such as the size, medium, and complexity of artwork when comparing prices.

Cash Flow Management

Managing cash flow effectively is critical for maintaining financial stability and ensuring that your art business can operate smoothly. Monitor your cash flow regularly to track incoming and outgoing funds, anticipate fluctuations, and manage liquidity effectively.

- Cash Flow Forecasting: Create a cash flow forecast to predict your future income and expenses based on historical data and projections. Anticipate seasonal fluctuations, irregular income sources, and potential expenses to ensure that you have sufficient funds to cover your financial obligations.

- Payment Terms and Policies: Establish clear payment terms and policies for your art sales, including accepted payment methods, deposit requirements, and payment deadlines. Communicate your payment terms to clients upfront to avoid misunderstandings and ensure timely payment for your work.

- Invoice Management: Issue invoices promptly for artwork sold and track payments received from clients. Follow up on overdue invoices and late payments to maintain positive cash flow and minimize financial disruptions.

Tax Planning and Compliance

Understanding tax obligations and compliance requirements is essential for artists to avoid penalties and ensure that they are meeting their tax obligations. Develop a tax planning strategy and work with a qualified accountant or tax professional to manage your tax affairs effectively.

- Tax Deductions: Take advantage of tax deductions available to artists, such as deductions for art supplies, studio expenses, travel costs, and marketing expenses. Keep detailed records of your expenses and consult with a tax professional to maximize your deductions and minimize your tax liability.

- Sales Tax Compliance: Understand the sales tax laws and regulations in your jurisdiction and ensure that you are collecting and remitting sales tax on art sales as required. Register for a sales tax permit if necessary and comply with filing deadlines and reporting requirements to avoid penalties.

- Estimated Tax Payments: If you are self-employed or have income from sources other than traditional employment, consider making estimated tax payments throughout the year to avoid underpayment penalties and ensure that you are meeting your tax obligations.

By implementing sound financial management practices, including budgeting and planning, pricing strategy, cash flow management, and tax planning and compliance, artists can achieve greater financial stability, support their artistic endeavors, and build a solid foundation for long-term success in the art business. Remember to regularly review and adjust your financial strategies as needed to adapt to changes in your circumstances and the art market.

Chapter 14: The Future of Selling Art

The landscape of art sales is constantly evolving, driven by advancements in technology, changes in consumer behavior, and shifts in the global marketplace. In this chapter, we'll explore emerging trends and developments shaping the future of selling art and discuss how artists can adapt and thrive in this ever-changing environment.

Digital Transformation and Online Sales

The rise of digital technology has revolutionized the way art is bought and sold, with online sales platforms and digital marketplaces offering artists unprecedented opportunities to reach global audiences and sell their artwork directly to collectors.

- Online Marketplaces: Online marketplaces such as Saatchi Art, Artsy, and Etsy have democratized the art market, making it easier for artists to showcase and sell their work to a global audience. Artists can leverage these platforms to reach collectors worldwide, bypassing traditional gallery channels and earning higher margins on their sales.

- Blockchain and NFTs: Blockchain technology and non-fungible tokens (NFTs) have emerged as new tools for buying, selling, and collecting digital art. NFTs allow artists to create unique, verifiable digital assets that can be bought, sold, and traded on blockchain-based platforms, opening up new opportunities for monetizing digital artwork and reaching digital art collectors.

- Augmented Reality (AR) and Virtual Reality (VR): Augmented reality and virtual reality technologies are transforming the way art is experienced and purchased online. Artists can use AR and VR to create immersive digital galleries and virtual exhibitions, allowing collectors to view and interact with artwork in a virtual environment before making a purchase.

Personalization and Customization

As consumer preferences continue to shift towards personalized and unique experiences, artists can differentiate themselves by offering personalized and customized artwork tailored to individual tastes and preferences.

- Custom Commissions: Offering commission-based services allows artists to create bespoke artwork that reflects the personal preferences and interests of individual clients. Whether it's a custom portrait, personalized painting, or bespoke illustration, custom commissions provide artists with opportunities to engage directly with collectors and create meaningful connections through art.

- Artisanal Craftsmanship: In an age of mass production and digital reproduction, there is a growing appreciation for artisanal craftsmanship and handmade goods. Artists can capitalize on this trend by emphasizing the unique qualities and craftsmanship of their artwork, highlighting the value of handmade, one-of-a-kind pieces in an increasingly digital world.

Sustainability and Social Responsibility

As concerns about environmental sustainability and social responsibility continue to grow, artists can align their art businesses with values of sustainability, ethical production, and social impact.

- Eco-Friendly Practices: Adopting eco-friendly practices and using sustainable materials in art production can appeal to environmentally conscious consumers and differentiate artists as responsible stewards of the environment. Artists can explore alternative materials, reduce waste, and minimize their carbon footprint to create artwork that aligns with sustainability principles.

- Social Impact Initiatives: Artists can leverage their platform and influence to raise awareness about social issues and support charitable causes through art. Whether it's through fundraising events, charity auctions, or art-based activism, artists can use their artwork as a powerful tool for social change and philanthropy.

- Ethical Production and Fair Trade: Embracing ethical production practices and fair trade principles can help artists ensure that their artwork is produced ethically and sustainably. Artists can source materials responsibly, support fair trade organizations, and prioritize fair wages and working conditions for artisans and collaborators involved in the production process.

Adaptability and Innovation

In an increasingly dynamic and competitive art market, adaptability and innovation are key to staying relevant and thriving as an artist. Artists must be willing to embrace change, experiment with new technologies, and adapt their strategies to meet the evolving needs and preferences of collectors and buyers.

- Experimentation and Exploration: Encourage experimentation and exploration in your artistic practice, embracing new techniques, mediums, and technologies to push the boundaries of creativity and innovation. Stay curious, open-minded, and willing to take risks in your artmaking process, knowing that experimentation is essential for growth and evolution as an artist.

- Collaboration and Cross-Pollination: Collaborating with other artists, creatives, and experts from different disciplines can spark new ideas, foster innovation, and create opportunities for cross-pollination of ideas and perspectives. Look for opportunities to collaborate on projects, exhibitions, or creative ventures that challenge and inspire you to think differently about your art practice.

- Continuous Learning and Professional Development: Commit to lifelong learning and professional development as an artist, seeking out opportunities to expand your skills, knowledge, and expertise. Whether it's through workshops, courses, or mentorship programs, investing in your growth and development as an artist is essential for staying competitive and relevant in the art market.

By embracing digital transformation, personalization, sustainability, and innovation, artists can position themselves for success in the future of selling art. By staying adaptable, innovative, and responsive to changing trends and consumer preferences, artists can continue to thrive and make meaningful contributions to the art world for years to come.

Chapter 15: Continuous Learning and Growth

In the ever-evolving landscape of art sales, artists must embrace a mindset of continuous learning and growth to stay relevant, adapt to new challenges, and seize emerging opportunities. In this chapter, we'll explore the importance of lifelong learning, strategies for skill development, and the benefits of fostering a growth mindset in the pursuit of artistic and professional excellence.

Lifelong Learning in the Arts

Lifelong learning is the ongoing process of acquiring new knowledge, skills, and perspectives throughout one's life. In the arts, lifelong learning is essential for artists seeking to expand their creative horizons, refine their techniques, and evolve their artistic practice over time.

- Skill Development: Lifelong learning provides artists with opportunities to develop and refine their artistic skills, whether through formal education, workshops, mentorship programs, or self-directed study. By continuously honing their craft, artists can push the boundaries of their creativity and achieve mastery in their chosen medium.

- Exploration and Experimentation: Lifelong learning encourages artists to explore new ideas, experiment with different techniques, and push outside their comfort zones. By embracing curiosity and open-mindedness, artists can discover new avenues of expression and innovation in their artwork.

- Adaptation to Change: Lifelong learning equips artists with the adaptability and resilience needed to navigate changes in the art market, technological advancements, and shifts in artistic trends. By staying informed about industry developments and evolving their skills accordingly, artists can position themselves for long-term success in a dynamic and competitive landscape.

Strategies for Continuous Growth

To foster continuous growth and development as an artist, it's essential to adopt strategies and habits that support ongoing learning and skill enhancement. By incorporating these strategies into their practice, artists can cultivate a growth mindset and unlock their full potential as creative professionals.

- Set Learning Goals: Set specific, achievable learning goals for yourself, whether it's mastering a new technique, exploring a different artistic style, or learning a new tool or technology. Break down your goals into manageable steps and create a plan for achieving them over time.

- Seek Feedback and Critique: Seek feedback and critique from peers, mentors, and fellow artists to gain insights into your work and areas for improvement. Embrace constructive criticism as an opportunity for growth and use feedback to refine your artistic practice and elevate your work to new levels of excellence.

- Experiment and Take Risks: Embrace experimentation and take risks in your artistic practice, exploring new ideas, materials, and approaches to creativity. Allow yourself the freedom to fail and learn from mistakes, knowing that experimentation is an essential part of the creative process.

- Stay Curious and Open-Minded: Cultivate a sense of curiosity and open-mindedness in your approach to artmaking, continually seeking out new sources of inspiration, learning, and growth. Stay informed about developments in the art world, attend exhibitions, lectures, and workshops, and engage with other artists and creatives to expand your perspective and knowledge.

Embracing a Growth Mindset

A growth mindset is the belief that intelligence, abilities, and talents can be developed through dedication, effort, and learning. By embracing a growth mindset, artists can overcome obstacles, persevere in the face of challenges, and unlock their full potential as creative individuals.

- Embrace Challenges: Embrace challenges as opportunities for growth and learning, viewing setbacks and obstacles as temporary setbacks rather than insurmountable barriers. Approach challenges with resilience, determination, and a willingness to learn from failure.

- Cultivate Resilience: Cultivate resilience in the face of adversity, setbacks, and criticism, knowing that setbacks are a natural part of the creative process. Build resilience by maintaining a positive outlook, seeking support from peers and mentors, and focusing on solutions rather than dwelling on problems.

- Celebrate Progress: Celebrate your progress and accomplishments along your artistic journey, acknowledging the effort and dedication you've invested in your growth and development. Take pride in your achievements, no matter how small, and use them as motivation to continue pushing forward on your path to artistic excellence.

By embracing lifelong learning, adopting strategies for continuous growth, and cultivating a growth mindset, artists can unlock their full potential, expand their creative horizons, and achieve artistic and professional excellence in the ever-evolving world of art sales. In the chapters that follow, we'll delve deeper into the strategies and tactics you can employ to effectively market, promote, and sell your original artwork while fostering a culture of continuous learning and growth.

Appendix: Resources for Artists

In this appendix, you'll find a curated list of resources to support artists in their journey to success in the art sales industry. From online platforms for showcasing artwork to educational resources for skill development, these resources cover a range of topics relevant to artists looking to enhance their artistic practice and expand their reach in the art market.

1. Online Galleries and Art Marketplaces:
    - Saatchi Art: A leading online gallery that connects artists with collectors worldwide.
    - Artsy: An online platform for discovering, buying, and selling art from leading galleries and artists.
    - Artfinder: An online marketplace for original art, featuring a diverse selection of artwork from independent artists.

2. Social Media Platforms:
    - Instagram: A visual platform for sharing artwork, connecting with fellow artists, and engaging with followers.
    - Facebook: A social networking platform where artists can create dedicated pages to showcase their artwork and connect with fans.
    - X (formerly Twitter): A microblogging platform for sharing updates, news, and artwork with a global audience.
    - Pinterest: A visual discovery platform where artists can share inspiration, ideas, and artwork with a community of enthusiasts.

3. Online Learning Platforms:
    - Skillshare: An online learning community with courses on art, design, photography, and creative entrepreneurship.
    - Udemy: An online platform offering courses on a wide range of topics, including art, illustration, painting, and digital art.
    - Coursera: An online education platform with courses from top universities and institutions, covering various aspects of art and design.

4. Artist Associations and Organizations:
    - The Artist's Way: A book by Julia Cameron that provides guidance and inspiration for artists seeking to unleash their creativity and overcome creative blocks.
    - The Creative Habit: A book by Twyla Tharp that explores the habits and rituals of creative professionals and offers insights into cultivating a productive and fulfilling creative practice.

6. Podcasts and Interviews:
    - The Art Life: A podcast hosted by artists Grace Bonney and Meighan O'Toole, exploring the intersection of art, creativity, and entrepreneurship.
    - Artists Helping Artists: A podcast hosted by artist Leslie Saeta, featuring interviews with artists, experts, and industry professionals sharing insights and advice for artists.

7. Legal and Business Resources:
   - Volunteer Lawyers for the Arts: An organization providing pro bono legal services to artists and arts organizations.
   - Small Business Administration (SBA): A government agency offering resources and support for small businesses, including guidance on business planning, financing, and legal compliance.

8. Art Market Reports and Industry Insights:
   - Art Market Monitor: A website offering news, analysis, and insights into the global art market, including trends, sales data, and expert commentary.
   - Artnet News: A leading source for news, analysis, and market intelligence in the art world, covering auctions, exhibitions, and industry developments.

These resources serve as valuable tools and sources of inspiration for artists seeking to navigate the art sales industry, develop their skills, and achieve success in their artistic endeavors. Whether you're looking to showcase your artwork, expand your knowledge, or connect with fellow artists and enthusiasts, these resources offer a wealth of opportunities for growth and exploration.

Acknowledgements:

I would like to express my sincere gratitude to everyone who has contributed to the creation of this book about selling original artwork.

First and foremost, I want to thank all the artists whose dedication, passion, and creativity inspire others every day. Your commitment to your craft and willingness to share your knowledge and experiences have been instrumental in shaping the content of this book.

I extend my heartfelt appreciation to the art collectors and patrons who support artists and contribute to the vitality of the art community. Your enthusiasm for art and your generosity in supporting artists are truly commendable.

I am deeply grateful to the countless professionals working behind the scenes in the art industry, including gallery owners, curators, art dealers, and art educators. Your expertise, guidance, and tireless efforts play a crucial role in nurturing artistic talent and promoting cultural exchange.

I want to acknowledge the role of technology in shaping the modern art market and extending the reach of artists around the world. To all the developers, designers, and innovators who create platforms and tools that empower artists to showcase and sell their work online, thank you for your invaluable contributions.

I am thankful for the support of my family, friends, and colleagues who have encouraged me throughout the writing process. Your encouragement, feedback, and understanding have been a source of strength and inspiration.

Lastly, I want to express my appreciation to the readers of this book. It is my sincere hope that the information, insights, and strategies shared within these pages will empower you on your journey to success in selling your original artwork.

Thank you all for your support and inspiration.

Warm regards,
Eleanor Carter

About the Author:

Eleanor Carter is a passionate artist and entrepreneur with a deep love for creativity and innovation. Eleanor has spent years honing her craft and exploring various mediums of artistic expression.

When not immersed in the world of art and business, Eleanor enjoys road trips and car camping around the US. She currently resides in Chicago, IL with her partner Jo and their dog Keegan, where they continue to explore new avenues of creativity and pursue their passion for art.

Eleanor Carter is excited to share her knowledge and insights with readers and hopes to inspire fellow artists to embrace their creativity, pursue their dreams, and thrive in the ever-evolving landscape of the art world.

www.ingramcontent.com/pod-product-compliance
Lightning Source LLC
Chambersburg PA
CBHW070953220526
45471CB00007B/3015